Dear Parents and Educators,

Our 500 Questions Game Book was created for parents and children to have fun together while learning. The book presents material on math, literacy, science, music, social skills, nature, creativity and health – all fundamental to school success. Our questions are lively, enriching, and unique, and our bonus riddles add extra learning and laughter!

Building a child's confidence and enthusiasm for learning at an early age is key to future success. It is our sincere hope that the Learnalots™ will inspire children, and those who care for them, to learn something new every day.

– The Learnalot Team

What are germs:
bacteria or bugs?

Which fruit has more potassium:
bananas or oranges?

Which species is the tallest
tree in the world:
sequoia or redwood?

bacteria, bananas, redwood

Does feline refer to dog or cat?

Are anteaters related to
sloths or Siberian tigers?

Is a slumber party a sleepover
with friends, or a party where
people cut trees?

cat, sloths, sleepover with friends

3

Do strawberries have seeds on the inside or the outside?

How many triangle faces does a pyramid have: four or five?

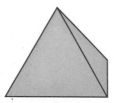

What sport do the Harlem Globetrotters play: baseball or basketball?

outside, four, basketball

Which state is the farthest south in the United States: Minnesota or Texas?

Do bagpipes come from South Africa or Scotland?

Which animals sleeps through the winter: hedgehogs or the hamsters?

Does accelerate mean to speed up or to slow down?

What is bigger: a crocodile or an alligator?

Is the sun made of hot gas or hot liquid?

speed up, crocodile, hot gas

If you have two dimes and a nickel, how much money do you have: 15 cents or 25 cents?

Do parrots like to imitate or irritate the sounds they hear?

Do olives grow on trees or bushes?

In which sport do you perform the butterfly stroke: tennis or swimming?

In which culture would you wear a lei around your neck: Hawaiian or Chinese?

Are crabs related to spiders or snakes?

swimming, Hawaiian, spiders

Is a cone a 2D shape
or a 3D shape?

Which word has the letter "U"
in it: kitty or puppy?

What do bees take from
flowers: nectar or nectarines?

Which instrument is used to measure temperature: a microscope or a thermometer?

Are adults closer to six feet tall or nine feet tall?

Is chocolate made from cocoa beans or cocoa bark?

thermometer, six feet, beans

Why do bees have sticky hair?

Because they use honeycombs!

Are storybooks written by an author or an illustrator?

Do rabbits eat plants or meat?

Which of these is likely magnetic: a boomerang or a pair of scissors?

Which state is the farthest north in the United States: California or Alaska?

Are kings thought of as regal or common?

What sense do you use when you are eating: sight or taste?

Alaska, regal, taste

Does sugar dissolve
or clump together when
you pour it in water?

Is an herbivore an animal
that eats plants or meats?

If an object is microscopic,
is it really tiny or really hot?

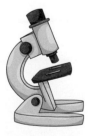

Which of these words is
a noun: sit or chair?

How many sides do most
snowflakes have: four or six?

Do snakes shed their
tails or their skin?

chair, six, skin

Does the sun rise in
the east or the west?

Is the
Eiffel Tower
located in
New York City
or Paris, France?

Which word has the letter W
in it: towel or shovel?

W

Which happens at the end of the day: sunset or sunrise?

What shape is Earth: a cone or a sphere?

Would a plumber fix your roof or your toilet?

sunset, sphere, toilet

Which animal can be
used for transportation:
a leopard or a camel?

Which bird lays the
largest egg in the world:
an ostrich or a penguin?

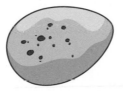

Do zoologists
study animals
or plants?

Are briefcases
used to
hold paper
or parakeets?

Which animal can't
stick out its tongue:
a crocodile or a chameleon?

Which part of your body
is important for balance:
your ears or your stomach?

paper, crocodile, ears

Is the Mariana Trench
a large cave or the
deepest place in the ocean?

Are picky eaters referred to
as finicky or winicky?

What is in the opposite direction
of west: south or east?

Which is the fastest dog in the world: the Greyhound or the Dalmatian?

How many legs do centipedes have: 6 or 100?

Do farmers work in agriculture or architecture?

Greyhound, 100, agriculture

What are
the strongest
creatures in
the ocean?

Mussels!

Which animals hold hands at night so they don't drift apart: otters or octopuses?

In the sport of bowling, does a strike refer to knocking down six pins or ten pins?

Is a bamboo stick really strong or really weak?

Does the taste of honey change depending on the flowers used to make it or the time of year it is made?

Do you get confidence from completing a task or quitting a task?

Are spiders arachnids or insects?

flowers, completing, arachnids

Which animal can hide inside
its shell for protection:
a sea turtle or a tortoise?

Which sea animal makes pearls:
an oyster or a sea cucumber?

Do genies
live in
a bottle
or a jar?

tortoise, oyster, bottle

Are a bird's bones hollow or solid?

Which is stronger than brick: wood or cement?

Does an umpire work at a sports game or a courtroom?

hollow, cement, sports game

Does gigantic mean
very small or very large?

Does accumulate mean
to collect or to give away?

Does Jack Frost
make snow
or ice cream?

very large, collect, snow

Which animal has webbed
wings: a bat or an owl?

Does cotton come from
a plant or an animal?

When two musicians
play together, is it called
a solo or a duet?

bat, plant, duet

Does checkers require
two players or four players?

Does evaporate mean to get
dirty or to turn water into gas?

Do sand dollars come from
sea urchins or sea stars?

If you were on a safari, would you ride in a boat or in a jeep?

Do piranha fish have sharp teeth or sharp noses?

Does silk come from worms or from snakes?

jeep, sharp teeth, worms

Does bath water get hotter or colder the longer you sit in it?

Is the pupil a part of your ears or your eyes?

Is a traditional Hawaiian party called a luau or an aloha?

colder, eyes, luau

33

What sport is a combination of soccer and baseball: softball or kickball?

Which is larger: a boat or a ship?

Does absorb mean to soak up liquid or to leak liquid?

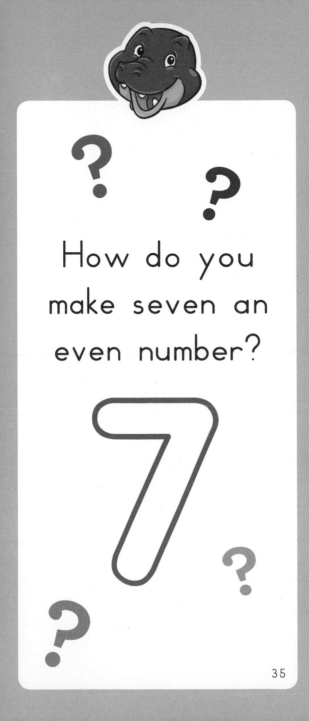

How do you make seven an even number?

You take
the "S"
off!

Are fossils at least
100 years old or at least
10,000 years old?

Are dinosaur bones
ancient or modern?

Which animal has four
stomachs: cows or koalas?

What do you call the moon when it is a big, bright circle: a new moon or a full moon?

Is a salamander a lizard or a bird?

Does multiply mean to increase or to decrease?

Is California a
state or a country?

Does the constellation Ursa Major
mean big gorilla or big bear?

Do caterpillars have 12 eyes or 2?

state, big bear, 12

Does incline refer to
an upward angle or
a downward angle?

Which letter is a consonant:
I or J?

Do sneezes occur in
your sinus or throat?

upward, J, sinus

Which continent is also a
country: Canada or Australia?

Which word has more A's:
abracadabra or Argentina?

Which animal is said to be
able to predict the end of
winter: a bear or a groundhog?

Which liquid do humans need to survive: milk or water?

What does "amigo" mean in the Spanish language: friend or taco?

Which animal lives in the water: a possum or an otter?

water, friend, otter

Does a biologist study rocks or living things?

Which animal has longer ears: a rabbit or a cat?

Which is the biggest desert in the world: the Sahara or the Arabian?

living things, rabbit, Sahara

43

Is Thanksgiving in the fall
or in the spring?

Is tea made from
plants or animals?

What color is your blood:
blue or red?

fall, plants, red

How long does it take for the moon to go around the Earth: one month or one year?

Were sandwiches invented by the Earl of Sandcastle or the Earl of Sandwich?

Which animal is nocturnal: a bat or a crow?

If you cut a pizza into thirds,
do you have two pieces
or three pieces?

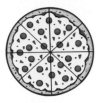

Do hedgehogs have
poor eyesight or poor smell?

Does the Earth rotate around
the sun, or does the sun
rotate around the Earth?

three, eyesight, Earth rotates around the sun

Why do birds
fly south for
the winter?

47

Because it's too far to walk.

Do people get goosebumps when they are hot or when they are cold?

Is spaghetti sauce made from tomatoes or strawberries?

How many teeth do most adults have: 32 or 52?

cold, tomatoes, 32

Do ladybugs eat aphids or apples?

Which country is known
for having a lot of windmills:
The Netherlands or Canada?

Which is closer to earth:
the moon or the sun?

aphids, The Netherlands, moon

When someone dresses up, do they look fabulous or delicious?

What is a passport used for: traveling outside the country or checking out books from the library?

Is the bow of the boat the front of the boat or the back of the boat?

Would you use a telescope to look at constellations or mold?

Do armadillos have sharp spikes or a hard shell on their backs?

Which is the only food that never spoils: honey or chicken?

constellations, hard shell, honey

Is a frog a reptile
or an amphibian?

How many days are in
a year: 275 or 365?

Do frilled lizards open their frills
to scare predators or catch bugs?

amphibian, 365, scare predators

Do giraffes clean
theirs ears
with their tongues
or their tails?

What is used to keep a boat in
place: the brakes or an anchor?

Does hyperactive mean
high energy or low energy?

Does inflate mean
to fill or to empty?

What do you call a female pig:
a sow or a boar?

Is a baby fox called
a kit or a chick?

Do bats sleep right-side up
or upside down?

Which of these is a type
of vegetable: a cucumber
or a cuckooflower?

Is a tiny cabbage known as a
Brussels sprout or potato sprout?

56 upside down, cucumber, Brussels sprout

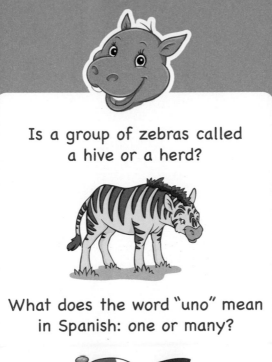

Is a group of zebras called
a hive or a herd?

What does the word "uno" mean
in Spanish: one or many?

Is a lyre a garden tool
or an instrument?

herd, one, instrument

Is the longest river in the United States the Missouri or the Mississippi?

What do you call an airplane that can land on the water: a seaplane or a sailplane?

Does a porcupine have spikes or quills?

Missouri, seaplane, quills

What did
the tie say
to the hat?

You go
on ahead
and I'll
hang around.

Is gold made from chemicals
or dug from the ground?

What grows faster:
your hair or your fingernails?

What should you drink to prevent
heatstroke: soda or water?

dug from the ground, hair, water

Do supermodels walk on a catwalk or a dogwalk?

Are jellybeans grown in a garden or made in a factory?

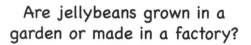

If a job is called a "piece of cake" is it going to be easy or difficult?

catwalk, made in a factory, easy

Does fire require oxygen
or helium to burn?

Do horses have the largest
eyes or the largest teeth
of any land animal?

Are robots complex
or simple machines?

oxygen, eyes, complex

63

What can happen if
you don't sleep enough:
you grow taller or you get sick?

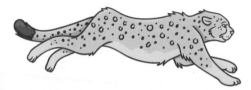

Do spiders
lay eggs or
give birth?

Which is the fastest animal
in the world: the cheetah
or the jaguar?

Do snowshoes look more like
tennis rackets or hockey sticks?

Which part of the Earth
supports the continents:
the crust or the mantle?

Does maple syrup come from
a tree or an animal?

tennis rackets, crust, tree

Before pens were invented, did people write with quills and ink or berries and sticks?

Is a bookworm someone who likes to read or someone who likes to wiggle?

Which animal can see behind themselves without turning their heads: a rabbit or a wolf?

quills and ink, read, rabbit

Does a hurricane have a "tooth" or an "eye"?

Who is the leader of the United States: the senator or the president?

Is a butterfly a crustacean or insect?

eye, president, insect

67

Does toothpaste contain
flour or fluoride?

Do tomatoes grow on
a bush or a tree?

Are boas made of
fur or feathers?

fluoride, bush, feathers

Do ants live as a group in a colony or alone by themselves?

Does submerge mean to descend below water or rise up above water?

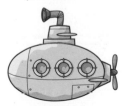

Do acorns grow on trees or bushes?

Which flavor are cats not able to taste: sweet or salty?

Do firefighters use arrows or axes to get into burning houses?

Which animal has teeth that never stop growing: a horse or a beaver?

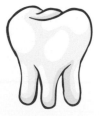

sweet, axes, beavers

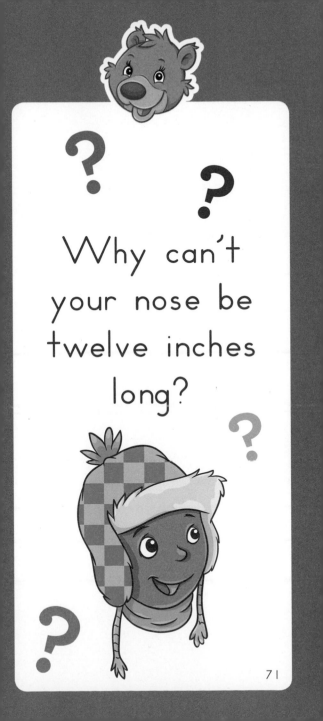

Why can't your nose be twelve inches long?

Because then
it would
be a foot!

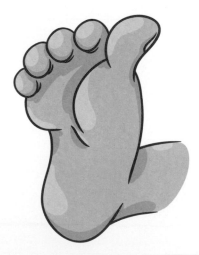

If you round 264 to the nearest ten, do you get 260 or 270?

Is the world's stinkiest cheese from Finland or from France?

Which of these is an animal: coral or a mushroom?

260, France, coral

73

Which can you hear:
fog or hail?

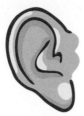

Which plant is found in a pond:
a cactus or a cattail?

Are baby camels born
with or without humps?

hail, cattail, without

Are stars made
out of gas or rock?

Do bears eat
blueberries or grapes?

Which gender of toad croaks:
the male or the female?

gas, blueberries, male

Which part
of a plant
soaks up water:
the flowers
or roots?

Do you wash your hands
to keep them soft or
to prevent getting sick?

Which is the
fastest animal
that runs on
two legs:
an ostrich
or a flamingo?

roots, prevent getting sick, ostrich

What does "hola" mean
in the Spanish language:
please or hello?

Is there more water or more
land on the Earth's surface?

Are dogs known as man's
best find or man's best friend?

hello, water, friend

Which is greater: 1111 or 1001?

How many states are there in the United States: 40 or 50?

What is the very center of a target called: the bull's eye or the cat's eye?

Which is attracted to a magnet: a pencil or a nail?

Is the city of Tokyo in Japan or China?

What do you get when you crush and grind grain: flour or sugar?

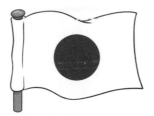

nail, Japan, flour

Is yoga a type of exercise
or a type of furniture?

Is a shark a predator animal
or prey animal?

Do tiaras dizzle or dazzle?

exercise, predator, dazzle

What is the main ingredient in an omelet: eggs or potatoes?

Does an eagle have toenails or talons?

Does a river have a "nose" or a "mouth"?

eggs, talons, mouth

Which is earlier:
10am or 1pm?

How many strings
does a guitar
have: three
or six?

Which can run faster:
a human or a hippo?

10am, six, hippo

What did the
mother broom
say to the
baby broom?

It's time
to go
to sweep!

Does water freeze at
32 or 65 degrees Fahrenheit?

Which insect can jump the
highest: grasshoppers or ants?

Are totem poles carved
out of soap or wood?

32, grasshoppers, wood

Are balloons made out of rubber or wrapping paper?

Can bears see really far or smell really well?

Is a whale a mammal or a fish?

rubber, smell really well, mammal

Is a baby goat
called a pup or a kid?

Do teeth have roots or retinas?

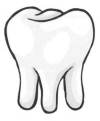

Which of these fruits have pits:
peaches or kiwis?

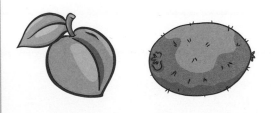

Do humans breathe
helium or oxygen?

Is a banana split a type of
dessert or a gymnastics move?

What do people eat at
Halloween: caramel cranberries
or caramel apples?

oxygen, dessert, caramel apples

Do fruits and vegetables
contain lots of fat or
lots of vitamins?

Do snails leave behind a trail
of mud or a trail of mucus?

Does jumping on a trampoline
cause your body to burn pixels
or to burn calories?

vitamins, mucus, calories

Does the word "timber" refer to rubber or wood?

Do crabs have a skeleton on the inside or outside of their bodies?

Who is known to have discovered mixing colors to form a new color: Plato or Pluto?

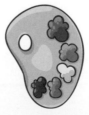

wood, outside, Plato

Are octopuses really smart
or really furry animals?

Does solar refer to
the sun or the moon?

What do you call a play
that has songs in it:
a musical or a tragedy?

smart, sun, musical

Is basketball played on
a court or on a field?

Does clay come from
a tree or from the ground?

Do hummingbirds make
a humming sound with
their wings or beaks?

court, ground, wings

Do bellhops work at hotels or hospitals?

Do people pay for groceries at a recorder or at a register?

In the French language, does "Bonjour" mean "I'm sorry" or "hello"?

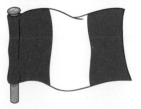

hotels, register, hello

Are pyramids found in France or Egypt?

Does gravity pull objects up toward the sky or down toward the ground?

Which mineral is known as being the hardest: emeralds or diamonds?

Egypt, down, diamonds

What do you call a pig that does karate?

95

Porkchop!

Is a baby horse called
a foal or a lamb?

"Umbrella" in the Latin language
refers to what word:
rain or shade?

Which city is the
Golden Gate Bridge in:
Chicago or San Francisco?

foal, shade, San Francisco

Which of these animals has feathers: a viper or a vulture?

Which animal falls asleep standing up: a horse or a hedgehog?

Which number is greater than 1000: 999 or 1001?

Which word has more p's:
pepper or purple?

P

What is faster:
a helicopter or a car?

Which tree is used
for Christmas trees:
an evergreen or a maple?

Which instrument family
does the trumpet belong to:
the brass or the woodwind?

How many stars are on the
American flag: 30 or 50?

Which word rhymes
with toe: how or row?

brass, 50, row

Which animal has the
largest eyes in the world:
a squid or a whale?

Does a bowling ball weigh closer
to 15 pounds or 50 pounds?

Are clouds made of tiny
water drops or tiny tear drops?

squid, 15, water

Do daydreams happen when you are awake or when you are asleep?

Does water flow downhill or uphill?

As a candle burns, does it grow or shrink?

awake, downhill, shrink

Is the center of the Earth
really cold or really hot?

Do sloths live in
jungles or in deserts?

Do whales have lungs or gills?

Is the moon one temperature or does it change between hot and cold?

Which are stronger: your arms or your legs?

How long would it take to fly to Mars in a rocket: seven days or seven months?

it changes, legs, seven months

Which fish is used the most to make sushi: tuna or barracuda?

Who can see better at night: people or cats?

Which of these phrases is correct: "righty tighty, lefty loosey", or "righty mighty, lefty goosey"?

tuna, cats, righty tighty, lefty loosey

How fast can race cars go:
120 mph or 220 mph?

Do rivers flow into oceans,
or do oceans flow into rivers?

Is the esophagus
in your throat or ear?

220 mph, rivers flow into oceans, throat

What did the fish name his son?

Gill!

Which of these words is another word for surprise: startle or soothe?

Is your tongue the weakest or strongest muscle in your body?

Are giraffe legs around 6 feet tall or 12 feet tall?

startle, strongest, 6

Is a car closer to
15 feet long or 50 feet long?

Which animals don't have
brains: starfish or crabs?

Is a baby elephant called
a calf or a foal?

15 feet, starfish, calf

Is a tambourine a percussion instrument or a string instrument?

Is honeydew a fruit or a flower?

Are diamonds formed deep under ground from high pressure or above ground from low pressure?

percussion, fruit, high pressure

What do you call the liquid inside of a coconut: milk or juice?

Do police officers give tickets for driving too fast or for singing too loud?

Do peaches have many seeds inside or one big pit?

milk, driving fast, one big pit

Are beavers
rodents or canines?

Does PB&J stand for
peanut butter and jelly,
or pickles, bacon, and juice?

How much money would
it take to buy a car:
100 dollars or 10,000 dollars?

rodents, peanut butter and jelly, 10,000 dollars

Is the biggest state in America
Rhode Island or Alaska?

Which animal is nocturnal:
a raccoon or a squirrel?

Is a fold-up up bed
called a kit or a cot?

Alaska, raccoon, cot

Which is the largest shark in the world: the whale shark or the great white shark?

Which of these has seeds: watermelons or carrots?

Are ballerinas graceful or clumsy?

whale shark, watermelons, graceful

Which animal can't move its eyeballs: an owl or a bat?

Which material would a t-shirt be made from: cornstarch or cotton?

What kind of scientist studies dinosaurs: a physiologist or a paleontologist?

owl, cotton, paleontologist

Is the smartest animal
a monkey or a dog?

Do skunks protect themselves
from predators by hiding in a
shell or spraying a stinky scent?

Which of
these words
is a verb:
swim or
swimsuit?

monkey, spraying, swim

117

Is Mexico a country in
North America or South America?

Is a person who
studies planets and space
an astronomer or an astronaut?

To watch a bird in a tall tree,
should you use binoculars
or a magnifying glass?

North America, astronomer, binoculars

What did the pirate say on his 80th birthday?

Aye Matey!

80

Is a Mohawk a type of
hairstyle or a type of bird?

Which dinosaur had three horns:
ankylosaurus or triceratops?

Is a group of wolves
called a pride or a pack?

Is pottery made
from plastic or clay?

What kind of animals
would you see at a zoo's
raptor show: birds or seals?

Is the
Statue of Liberty
made of
gold or copper?

clay, birds, copper

If you cut an apple into
quarters, how many pieces
would you have: two or four?

Are mangoes an exotic fruit
or a hypnotic fruit?

Does beachcomb mean to look for
shells, or put sand in your hair?

Does a grasshopper or a butterfly hatch from a chrysalis?

Which are bigger: trolls or giants?

Which is a unit of weight: a kilometer or kilogram?

butterfly, giants, kilogram

Which of these is a type of cloud: nimbus or newton?

Do leprechauns hide gold at the end of rainbows or the end of rivers?

Are omnivores animals that eat plants, meat, or both plants and meat?

nimbus, rainbows, plants and meat

Which is colder:
the North Pole or South Pole?

Do lions live in Asia or Africa?

Is the width of the United
States (coast to coast) roughly
270 miles or roughly 2,700 miles?

South Pole, Africa, 2,700 miles

Is a cartwheel a gymnastics move or a carnival ride?

Which word has the letter D at the end: sad or sat?

D

Do your lungs help you digest food or help you breathe?

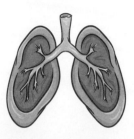

gymnastics move, sad, breathe

Is light and fluffy snow
known as slush or powder?

What is a ray of light
from the moon called:
a moonstream or a moonbeam?

Do trees produce
oxygen or carbon dioxide?

powder, moonbeam, oxygen

Do birds fly in an
arrow shape or circle shape?

Do all spiders have
eight legs or six legs?

How many hours
are in a day: 15 or 24?

arrow, eight, 24

Which time is the same as a quarter past two: 2:15 or 2:30?

Does a deer have horns or antlers?

Is a bat a bird or a mammal?

2:15, antlers, mammal

What did the
beaver say to
the tree?

131

It's been nice
gnawing you!

How many legs would a team of four horses have: 15 or 16?

Do tractors paddle the ground or plow the ground?

Do sharks have bones or cartilage in their bodies?

16, plow, cartilage

Do peanuts grow above
ground or under ground?

Do kangaroos live
in Australia or Africa?

Can trees live for hundreds of
years or thousands of years?

underground, Australia, thousands

Which direction is the
opposite of east: north or west?

When someone says it's
raining cats and dogs,
do they mean it is raining hard,
or they see animals in the sky?

Do male elk shed their antlers
every year or every month?

west, raining hard, every year

Which dinosaur was known to fly: stegosaurus or pterodactyl?

Which ocean is smaller: the Atlantic or the Pacific?

Who painted the Mona Lisa: Leonardo da Vinci or Ludwig von Beethoven?

pterodactyl, Atlantic, da Vinci

Which melts ice faster:
sugar or salt?

Is a beet a fruit or vegetable?

Does the earth have
four seasons or six?

salt, vegetable, four

Which state are oranges
grown in: Minnesota or Florida?

Is Monday part of
a weekend or a weekday?

Do cherries grow
on trees or bushes?

Florida, weekday, trees

What is larger:
a violin or a cello?

Which planet has rings:
Saturn or Mars?

Are the holes on the
surface of the moon called
critters or craters?

cello, Saturn, craters

Which dinosaur had
sharp plates on its back:
apatosaurus or stegosaurus?

What part of corn do we eat:
the seeds or the leaves?

Which animal is known
to show emotions:
grasshoppers or gorillas?

stegosaurus, seeds, gorillas

Is an eclipse when the moon blocks the sun or when Mercury block the sun?

Is a group of turtles called a bunch or a bale?

How many planets are in the solar system: eight or ten?

moon, bale, eight

What animal helps to pollinate flowers: a bear or a bee?

Do beaver dams create ponds or lakes?

Does dinosaur mean "terrible lizard" or "hungry lizard?"

bee, ponds, terrible lizard

Why are ghosts bad liars?

143

Because you can see right through them!

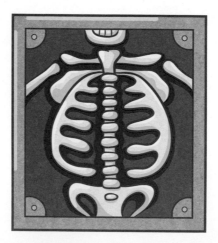

Do pilots work
in advertising
or aviation?

Which holiday is
celebrated with a menorah:
Easter or Hanukkah?

How many lungs do
you have: two or four?

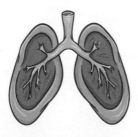

If you have 6 pairs of socks, do you have 14 or 12 individual socks?

Where is the Amazon River: in Belgium or Brazil?

In what sport do you jump on a trampoline: gymnastics or karate?

12, Brazil, gymnastics

Do flowers start to bloom
in November or May?

Does water boil at 212
or 85 degrees Fahrenheit?

Do rivers grow when
snow falls or when snow melts?

May, 212, melts

Does cheese come from
goats or groundhogs?

Which dinosaur was bigger: a
tyrannosaurus or a velociraptor?

Which animal is a predator to
penguins: seals or polar bears?

goats, tyrannosaurus, seals

Who watches a penguin chick
when it is first born:
the mother or the father?

Does the U.S. President live in the
White House or Orange House?

Do hermit crabs keep their
shells for life or find new ones
as they grow?

father, White House, new ones

How long does it take for light to travel from the sun to Earth: eight minutes or eight days?

Is karate a type of modern art or martial art?

Is a traditional Hawaiian dance called a hula or a tuba?

eight minutes, martial art, hula

Does corn grow on
a stalk or a trunk?

What time is it if it is
three hours after ten o'clock:
one or two o'clock?

Which state is larger:
Texas or Alaska?

stalk, one, Alaska

151

Do blackberry bushes
have thorns or smooth vines?

Which planet is red:
Mars or Jupiter?

Was skiing
invented in
Canada or
Norway?

thorns, Mars, Norway

Which animals get sunburned: pigs or cows?

Which animal burrows underground: a squirrel or a groundhog?

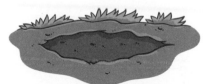

What is the opposite of wild: crazy or tame?

pigs, groundhog, tame

Are airplanes aerobic
or aerodynamic?

What is the deepest part
of the Earth called:
the crust or the core?

How many teeth does an
alligator have: 10 or 80?

aerodynamic, core, 80

Don't look
now, but
there's
something
smelly
between us!

Is the longest day in
the summer or the winter?

Are plastic bottles made
from tree sap or from
oil deep underground?

Which of these was
invented first: the light bulb
or the microwave?

Is lightning a discharge of electricity or a discharge of fire?

Do cupcakes contain more salt or sugar?

Does poison ivy grow in the forest or at the beach?

electricity, sugar, forest

Is a mushroom a type of plant
or a type of fungus?

Which is the biggest country in
the world: China or Russia?

Is the earth spinning:
yes or no?

fungus, Russia, yes

159

Is Earth five billion or
five thousand years old?

Are clogs worn in China
or the Netherlands?

Have astronauts landed
on Jupiter or on the moon?

five billion years, Netherlands, moon

What is another word for flower: blossom or leaf?

Are pirates known as robbers of the salt or robbers of the sea?

Do flying helicopters detect nearby aircraft using sonar or radar?

Is bluegrass a type of food
or a type of music?

Are cranberries
tart or sweet?

Is a moose's favorite food
grass or caterpillars?

music, tart, grass

Does an animal's heart slow down when it is hibernating or hunting?

What animal lives longer: a mouse or a sea turtle?

Do butterflies hatch from a chrysalis or a crystal?

hibernating, sea turtle, chrysalis

163

Does the word "sidekick" refer to a good friend or an enemy?

What is a scientist called that studies rocks and minerals: a geologist or a meteorologist?

Which country has a maple leaf on its flag: Canada or Mexico?

good friend, geologist, Canada

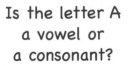

Is the letter A
a vowel or
a consonant?

Do dogs cool down
by panting or sweating?

Does a
policeman
enforce the laws
or make the laws?

vowel, panting, enforce the laws

How many points do most starfish have: five or eight?

Is a ballroom a room for dancing or a room for bouncing balls?

Are grandmothers your mother's sister or your mother's mom?

five, dancing, mother's mom

If you were in a race and passed the person in second place, what place would you be in?

Second place!

Do the blue parts on a globe refer to water or land?

What month is Christmas in: December or September?

Which travels faster: light or sound?

water, December, light

169

What builds up on your teeth
and gives you cavities:
plaque or scales?

Which animal builds dams and
lodges: a beaver or an otter?

How many holes do bowling
balls have: three or five?

plaque, beaver, three

Which grows faster:
a bamboo tree or an oak tree?

Which of these is a plant:
a yucca or a ukulele?

When a bird flies south in
the winter, is it called
hibernation or migration?

bamboo, yucca, migration

When you reach a goal, do you feel triumphant or trumpeted?

Does the moon reflect light or absorb light?

Does the sun rise in the east or the south?

triumphant, reflect, east

Is the water
in a pond
moving
or still?

How many eggs are in
a half dozen: six or eight?

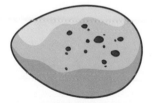

Which is a kind of dog:
a Siamese or a retriever?

still, six, retriever

Does an herbivore
eat plants or meat?

Is the biggest animal on
the planet a blue whale
or an elephant?

Is a group of lions called
a gang or a pride?

plants, blue whale, pride

Do people sneeze with
their eyes open or closed?

Does Bigfoot
live in a
forest or
in a jungle?

Are dogs reptiles or mammals?

closed, forest, mammals

Which language uses
"konnichiwa" to say hello:
Japanese or Russian?

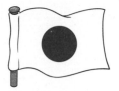

What would be an example
of precipitation: rain falling
from the sky or boiling water?

Is Australia known as
the country "Down Under"
or the country "Down Over"?

Japanese, falling rain, Down Under

Are canes used to walk with or to ski with?

Does divide mean to break apart or put together?

Does persistence mean: to keep trying or to give up easily?

walk, break apart, keep trying

Do mechanics
fix cars
or work
in hospitals?

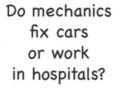

When fruit sits out for too long,
does it spoil or splatter?

Is a shark a fish or a mammal?

fix cars, spoil, fish

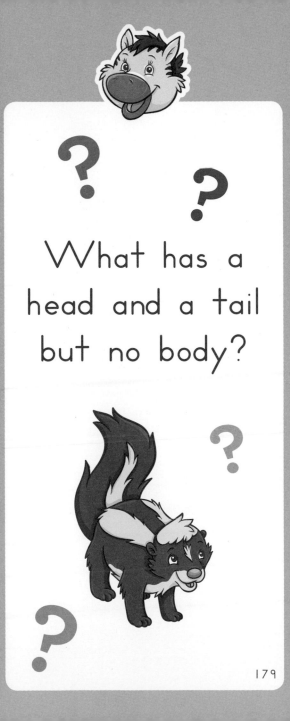

? **?**

What has a head and a tail but no body?

?

?

A coin!

Does irrigate mean to
water plants or to pick fruit?

How much sleep should
kids get each night:
six hours or ten hours?

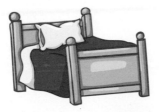

How much
exercise should
you get
every day:
10 minutes or
60 minutes?

water plants, ten hours, 60

Which insect lives in large colonies: ants or crickets?

Are bulls male cows or male goats?

Do you cross your fingers for good luck or when you make a wish?

ants, male cows, good luck

How many people live
in the United States:
120 million or 320 million?

How many days of the week
start with the letter "T":
two or three?

T

Is "perimeter" the distance
around the outside of a shape
or a type of fruit?

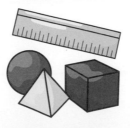

Does light enter a camera
through the lens or the flash?

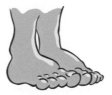

When you have no
shoes on, do you have
spare feet or bare feet?

What do you usually
see before a rainstorm:
dark clouds or sunshine?

lens, bare feet, clouds

What is 237 rounded to the nearest ten: 230 or 240?

237

Is your body made more of water or more of bone?

Which of these is an ocean: the Pacific or the Panama?

Which is larger, 1/4 or 1/6?

Are most flags square-shaped or rectangle-shaped?

Which birds get nectar from a flower: hummingbirds or robins?

1/4, rectangular, hummingbirds

Which fish can't blink its eyes:
a shark or a tuna?

Does a lily pad grow
in an ocean or a pond?

When is it more likely to snow:
January or July?

shark, pond, January

187

Which is longer:
an inch or a foot?

Before anchors were invented,
what was used to keep ships
in place: logs or rocks?

What part of a carrot do we
eat: the root or the leaves?

a foot, rocks, root

Is the planet Neptune
very hot or very cold?

How many continents are
there on Earth: 7 or 10?

How long does it take
for the Earth to travel
all the way around the Sun:
one month or one year?

very cold, 7, one year

Which of these is larger:
a teaspoon or a tablespoon?

Does rotate mean to
turn around or to cut in half?

Were triceratops
herbivores or omnivores?

tablespoon, turn around, herbivores

What has four
legs but
can't walk?

A chair!

Is the highest temperature in a home kitchen oven around 500 degrees F or 1000 degrees F?

Does ascend mean to go up or to go down?

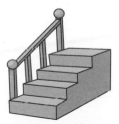

Do raisins come from grapes or oranges?

What are you more likely
to find in a hamburger:
a cucumber or a pickle?

Which city is known
as The Big Apple:
Sydney or New York?

Do engines give airplanes
thrush or thrust?

pickle, New York, thrust

Do wombats live
in Asia or Australia?

Which of these is
a pose in yoga:
shrub pose or tree pose?

Which is the most populated
city in the United States:
Los Angeles or New York?

Are baby sheep called
foals or lambs?

How many square faces
does a cube have: four or six?

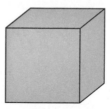

Is a wishbone part of the
elbow or collarbone in a turkey?

lambs, six, collarbone

Which of these is a secondary color: purple or yellow?

Do nurses work with pirates or patients?

Do doctors go to medical school or mechanic school?

What is harder:
a diamond or brick?

Does a carnivore eat
meat or plants?

Does a cat have
claws or talons?

diamond, meat, claws